SUPERHEROES SAY:

NO TO BULLYING

YES TO KINDNESS

LoLo Smith & Carla Nordé

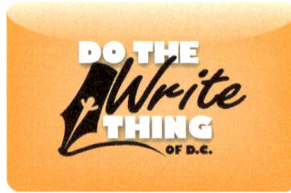

This book belongs to:

_____

Other Books for Children by LoLo Smith

Community Workers & COVID-19

I Know My Community Workers

Ten Acts of Kindness

My Doll & Me: Superheroes Fighting Bullying with Kindness

Max & Bo: Two Dogs On The Go

The Little Town of Share-A-Lot

Sista CindyElla Mae: The African-American Cinderella

All books are available at
amazon.com/author/lolosmith

Follow the author on social media:
facebook.com/lolo.smith.169405
Instagram: @lolosmith2016

Bullying has become a serious problem. Many children skip school every day because they are afraid they will be bullied.

All of us must help prevent bullying. We must stop saying unkind things to one another. We must stop fighting each other. We must stop being unkind to each other on the Internet. We must learn to be kind to one another. Kindness is the new cool!

When you see the word bully, think what the letters could stand for:

B BE A FRIEND!

U USE KIND WORDS!

L LOOK FOR AND REPORT BULLYING!

L LEARN TO UNDERSTAND OTHERS.

Y YOU CAN STOP BULLYING.

1

SUPERMAN & SUPERGIRL

want you
to learn about bullying.
They want you
to have a plan
to stop bullying
because bullying
is not okay.

2

THE FANTASTIC FOUR

(Mr. Fantastic, the Invisible Woman, the Human Torch & The Thing)

say there are four types of bullying:

1. Verbal bullying
2. Physical bullying
3. Social bullying
4. Cyber bullying

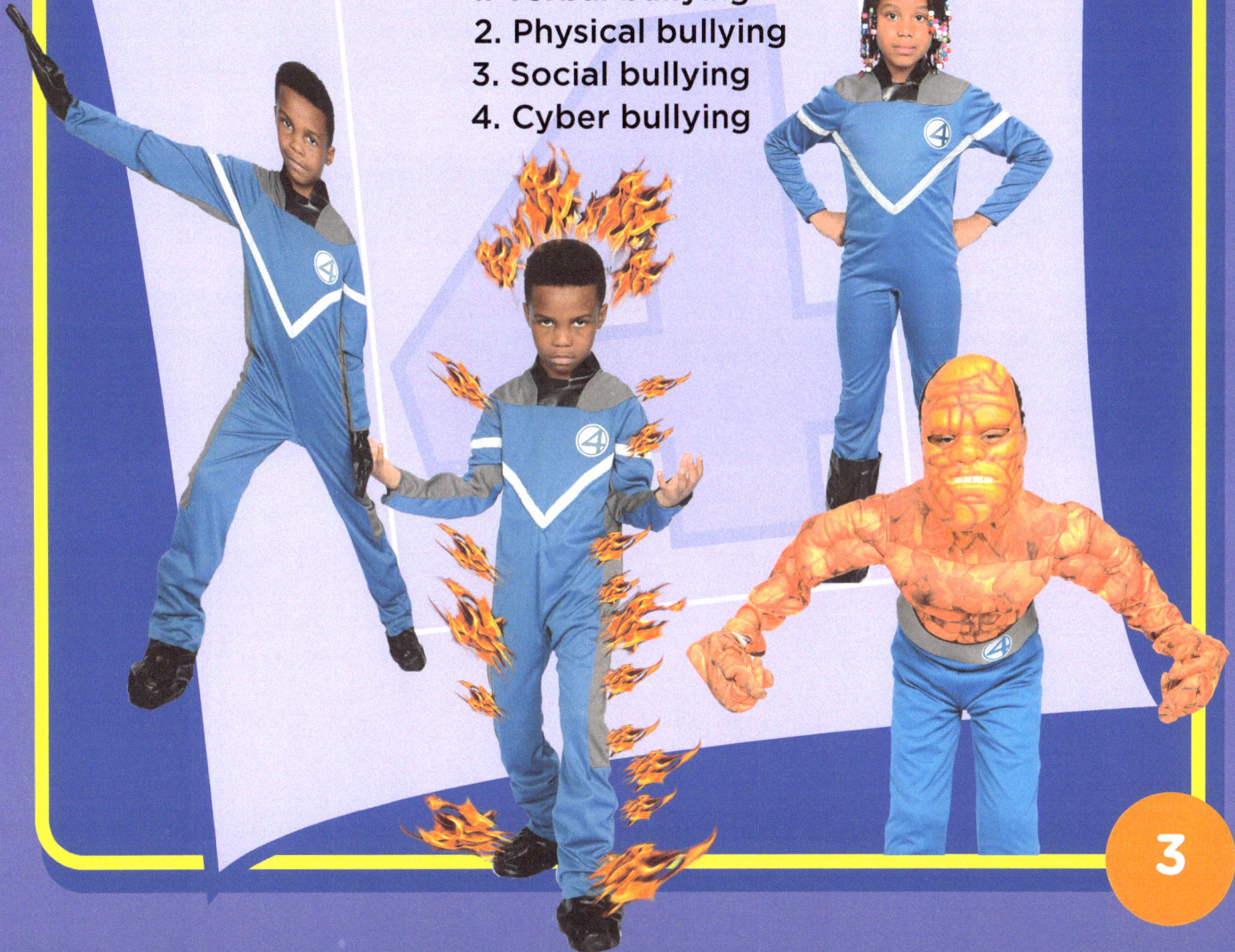

3

THE INCREDIBLES

The Incredibles *(Mister Incredible, Elastigirl, Violet, Dash and Jack-Jack)* say,

"Verbal bullying happens when a bully says unkind things to someone or about someone. A bully may also call you names. Bullying is not the same as friendly teasing."

4

CAPTAIN AMERICA & AMERICAN DREAM

say that **PHYSICAL** bullying means
hitting, spitting, kicking, pinching or throwing things.

5

SPIDER-MAN & SPIDERGIRL

say

SOCIAL bullying means leaving others out on purpose, spreading rumors or telling others not to be friends with someone.

WONDER WOMAN

teaches us about **CYBER** bullying.
She says to remember
to always use kind words
on the internet.
Don't be mean behind
the computer screen!

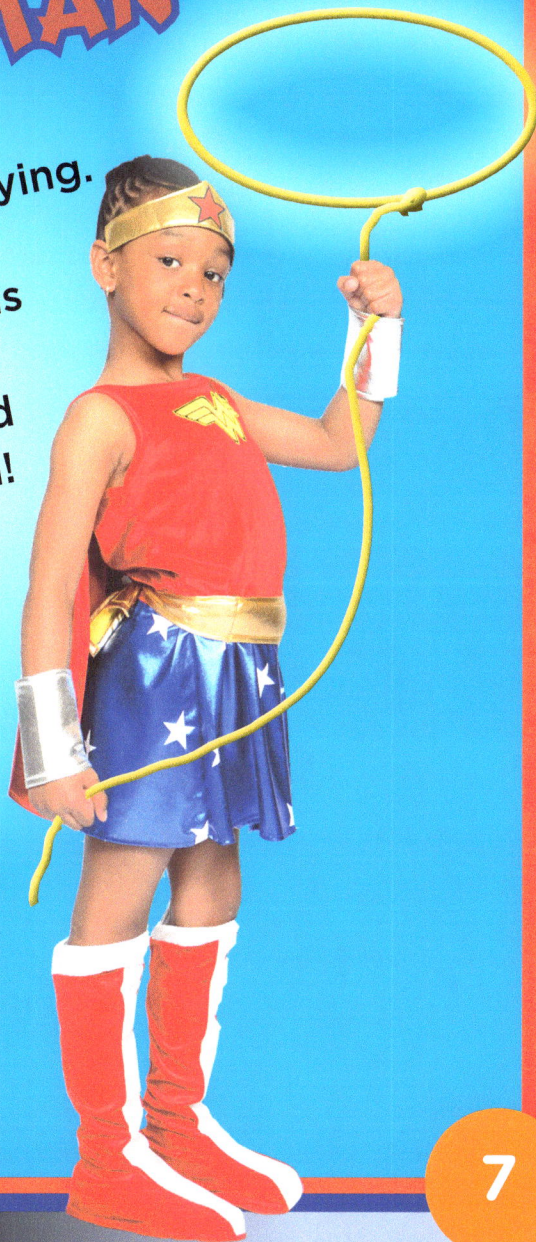

ROBIN

teaches us that there are **FOUR ROLES** that people play in a bullying situation:

1. The bully
2. The victim
3. The ally
4. The bystander

8

THE GREEN LANTERN & GREEN LANTERN GIRL

say that a **BULLY** is someone who tries to hurt others.
Bullies feel better by doing unkind things.
Bullies think they are cool. Bullies are not cool.
Be a buddy, not a bully.

9

HULK & SHE HULK

say that the **VICTIM** of bullying
is someone who is being called names,
being hit or being left out.
A victim may have trouble sleeping,
stop doing their work at school,
become sad, become afraid
or even want to stop living.

10

TEENAGE MUTANT NINJA TURTLES DONATELLO

say that a **VICTIM** can be any color, size or age.
It is okay to be different.
It is NOT okay to bully
someone for being different.

TEENAGE MUTANT NINJA TURTLES LEONARDO

say that **BYSTANDERS** do nothing to help a victim of bullying. That is wrong.

TEENAGE MUTANT NINJA TURTLES MICHELANGELO

say that the **ALLY** is a friend of the bully.
The ally is happy to see the bully hurt others.

TEENAGE MUTANT NINJA TURTLES RAPHAEL

say you should use the **TALK-WALK-TELL** strategy to deal with a bully.

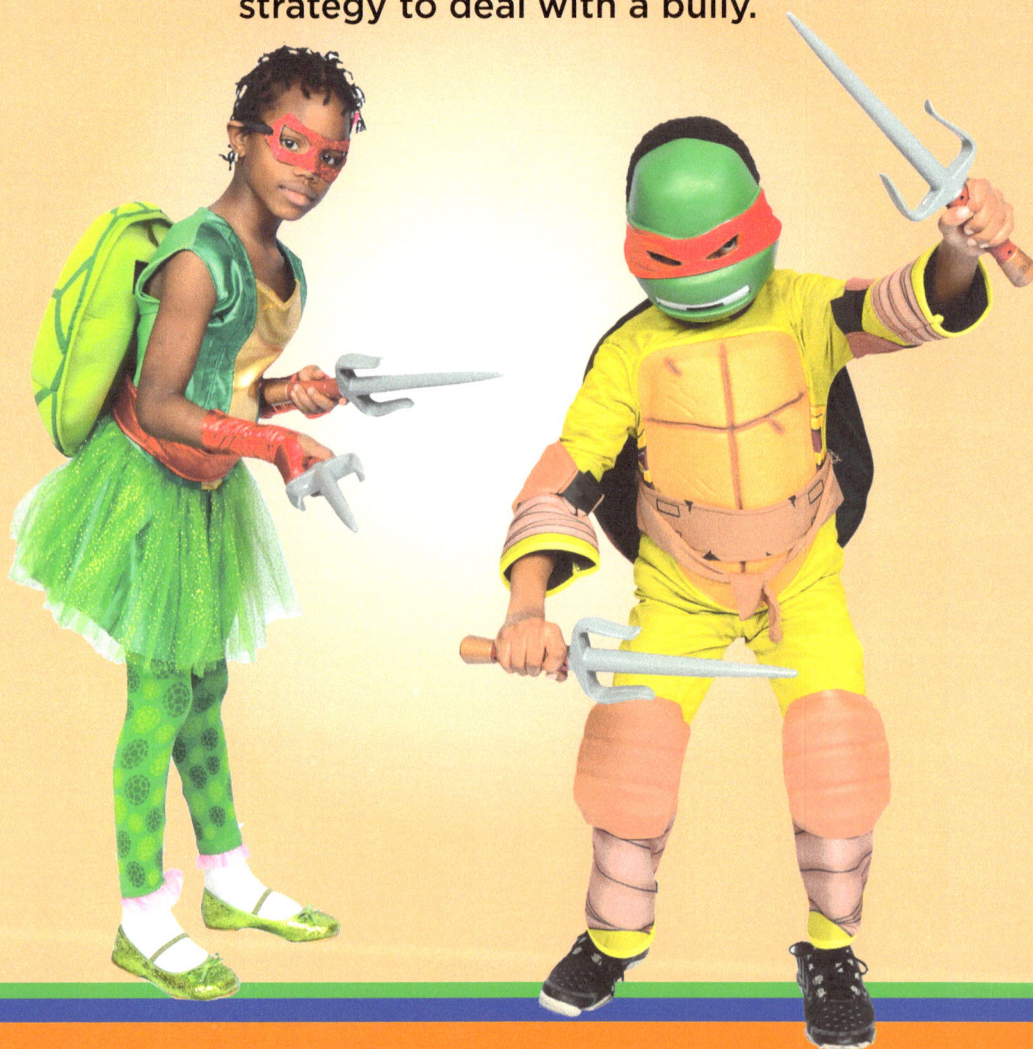

BATMAN & BATGIRL

say you should **TALK** to a bully and ask the bully to stop.

15

IRONMAN

says you can just
ignore a bully
and **WALK** away

16

THE FLASH & FLASH GIRL

say that if a bully does not stop, **TELL** your tell parent or your teacher. If you see something, say something. This is not tattling.

17

I PLEDGE TO SAY NO TO BULLYING!

☐ I pledge to stop bullying my sister or brother at home.

☐ I pledge to stop bullying other children at school.

☐ I pledge to stop bullying other children on the playground.

☐ I pledge to stop bullying on the Internet.

☐ I pledge to tell an adult when I see someone being bullied.

☐ I pledge to say no to bullying and be like a superhero.

_____

Name

(COPY THIS PLEDGE ON A SHEET OF PAPER)

10
ACTS OF KINDNESS

THE SUPERHEROES FIGHT BULLYING WITH KINDNESS.
When children act kind to one another,
bullying decreases in schools.
It does not cost anything to be kind.
On the following pages are 10 acts of kindness
that children and parents can try together.

ACT OF KINDNESS #1

Batman and Batgirl say,
"Use sidewalk chalk and write
kind messages on the sidewalk or parking lot
in your neighborhood."

A warm SMILE is the universal language of kindness.

GOOD LUCK :)

21

ACT OF KINDNESS #2

Captain America and American Dream say, "Think of three relatives that you do not see very often then write a nice, handwritten letter or card and drop it in the mail. Your letter or card will make them smile because it is rare to get a handwritten letter since most people just send texts or emails."

We RISE by lifting others.

23

ACT OF KINDNESS #3

The Flash and Flash Girl say,
"The next time that you are in a car,
wave and smile at people in other cars
to see if they will wave or smile back at you."

KINDNESS is free.

24

25

ACT OF KINDNESS #4

The Hulk and She Hulk say,
"Take flowers to your teacher.
They are much better than apples!"

Never look DOWN on someone unless you are helping them UP.

27

ACT OF KINDNESS #5

Wonder Woman says,
"If you have elderly neighbors,
check in on them and
ask if you can be of any help."

No act of
KINDNESS,
no matter how
SMALL,
is ever wasted.

29

ACT OF KINDNESS #6

Spider-Man and Spider Girl say,
"Share a special toy with a friend."

Choose
KINDNESS.

ACT OF KINDNESS #7

Robin says, "Ask a parent if they will take you to the children's hospital so you can donate your gently used toys."

KINDNESS is always in season.

TOYS

33

ACT OF KINDNESS #8

The Green Lantern and Green Lantern Girl say, "Make a thank you card for your teacher or principal."

One KIND WORD can change someone's ENTIRE DAY.

ACT OF KINDNESS #9

Superman and Supergirl say,
"Read a book
to a younger sister or brother."

KINDNESS
is the language
which the deaf
can HEAR and the
blind can SEE.

37

ACT OF KINDNESS #10

Iron Man says,
"You should invite a classmate who is easily left out, to play on the playground."

It's COOL to be KIND.

39

THE KINDNESS PLEDGE

☐ I pledge to be kind to my family at home.

☐ I pledge to be kind to my classmates at school.

☐ I pledge to be kind to my classmates
on the playground.

☐ I pledge to be kind to others on the Internet.

☐ I pledge to tell an adult when I see someone
being unkind.

☐ I pledge to be a buddy, not a bully.

_____
Name

(COPY THIS PLEDGE ON A SHEET OF PAPER)

JUST FOR FUN!

TRUE OR FALSE

1. Bullying is okay.

2. Bullying can only happen in a few places.

3. Bullying can happen at home, at school, on the playground and on the Internet.

4. A type of bullying is verbal bullying.

5. Bullying is the same thing as friendly teasing.

JUST FOR FUN

Point to the picture of the person who plays the roles in a bullying situation.

1. The person who is called names, being hit or being left out.

2. The person who tries to hurt others.

3. The person who stands by and does nothing when another person is being bullied.

4. The friend of the bully who is happy to see the bully being unkind to others.

Answers: 1. Victim 2. Bully 3. Bystander 4. Ally

Use this BINGO-style Kindness Game to help encourage your child to practice simple, yet powerful, acts of kindness.

Kindness BINGO

Use this BINGO style Kindness Game to help encourage your child to practice simple, yet powerful acts of kindness!

WRITE POSITIVE MESSAGES ON THE SIDEWALK	SAY THANK YOU TO COMMUNITY WORKERS	HOLD THE DOOR OPEN FOR SOMEONE	RETURN A SHOPPING CART TO DESIGNATED AREA	SHARE TOYS WITH FRIENDS
VISIT SICK CHILDREN	SMILE AT SOMEONE WALKING NEAR YOU	PLAY WITH LONELY KIDS	SHOVEL FOR YOUR NEIGHBOR WHEN IT SNOWS	TELL YOUR PRINCIPAL HOW GREAT YOUR TEACHER IS
SING SONGS AT A NURSING HOME	GIVE DONATIONS TO AN ORGANIZATION INSTEAD OF BIRTHDAY GIFTS	FREE SPACE	MAIL LETTERS TO PEOPLE	HELP SOMEONE BEING BULLIED
MAKE A THANK YOU SIGN FOR THE TRASH	WAVE TO PEOPLE IN CARS	GIVE FLOWERS TO TEACHERS	DONATE YOUR OLD	TELL YOUR PARENTS HOW

Kindness BINGO

Use this BINGO style Kindness Game to help encourage your child to practice simple, yet powerful acts of kindness!

BE A GOOD LISTENER	SEND THANK YOU NOTES	READ BOOKS FOR CHILDREN	HELP THE ELDERLY	DO A CHORE FOR SOMEONE WITHOUT THEM KNOWING
WRITE POSITIVE MESSAGES ON THE SIDEWALK	OFFER YOUR HELP TO SOMEONE WHO NEEDS IT	WAVE TO PEOPLE IN CARS	SHARE YOUR CANDY WITH YOUR FAMILY	SHARE TOYS WITH FRIENDS
VISIT SICK KIDS	GIVE A THANK YOU NOTE TO A LIBRARIAN	FREE SPACE	READ A BOOK TO SOMEONE	GIVE FOOD TO THE HOMELESS
RECYCLE	WRITE A POEM FOR	PLAY WITH LONELY KIDS	MAIL LETTERS TO PEOPLE	ADOPT A RESCUE PET
SAY THANK YOU TO THE MAILMAN				

Kindness BINGO

PLANT A TREE	VOLUNTEER	READ BOOKS FOR CHILDREN	HELP THE ELDERLY	PICK UP LITER AND THROW IT AWAY
WRITE POSITIVE MESSAGES ON THE SIDEWALK	SEND THANK YOU NOTES	OFFER YOUR SEAT TO AN ELDERLY PERSON ON A BUS	SHARE YOUR LUNCH WITH A FRIEND	SHARE TOYS WITH FRIENDS
VISIT SICK KIDS	SHARE FRUITS AND SNACKS WITH OTHER CHILDREN	FREE SPACE	DO SOMETHING TO SAVE THE PLANET	CALL YOUR GRANDPARENTS AND SAY HELLO
SMILE AT STRANGERS	GIVE A CARD TO SOMEONE IN THE HOSPITAL	PLAY WITH LONELY KIDS	MAIL LETTERS TO PEOPLE	SEND LETTERS TO OUR MILITARY
MAKE A THANK YOU SIGN FOR THE TRASH MAN	WAVE TO PEOPLE IN CARS	GIVE FLOWERS TO TEACHERS	PET A FRIENDLY DOG	FORGIVE SOMEONE YOU'RE UPSET WITH

Kindness BINGO

CHEER SOMEONE ON	SEND THANK YOU NOTES	TELL YOUR PARENTS HOW MUCH YOU LOVE THEM	VISIT SICK CHILDREN	COMPLIMENT SOMEONE
WRITE POSITIVE MESSAGES ON THE SIDEWALK	SAY THANK YOU TO COMMUNITY WORKERS	HOLD THE ELEVATOR FOR SOMEONE	RETURN A SHOPPING CART TO DESIGNATED AREA	GIVE FLOWERS TO TEACHERS
HELP THE ELDERLY	SMILE AT SOMEONE THAT WALKS NEAR YOU	FREE SPACE	WALK SOMEONE'S DOG	TELL YOUR PRINCIPAL HOW GREAT YOUR TEACHER IS
SING SONGS AT A NURSING HOME	TELL SOMEONE GOOD MORNING OR GOOD NIGHT	PLAY WITH LONELY KIDS	MAIL LETTERS TO PEOPLE	DONATE CLOTHING TO A SHELTER
MAKE A THANK YOU SIGN FOR THE TRASH MAN	WAVE AT PEOPLE IN CARS	SHARE TOYS WITH FRIENDS	DONATE YOUR OLD TOYS	READ BOOKS FOR CHILDREN

For FREE copies of these Bingo Sheets,
send email to: dothewritething1@gmail.com
Follow the author on social media:
facebook.com/lolo.smith.169405 and
Instagram @lolosmith2016

ABOUT THE AUTHORS

LoLo Smith is an educator, writer andcreatorof Living Storybook, a literacy and performing arts program for young children. She has written 8 books for children on topics such as bullying, kindness, careers, COVID-19 and holidays. Her books feature Anime characters, community workers, superheroes, American Girl dolls and even dogs! All of her books can be found at amazon.com/author/lolosmith.
Follow her on social media at facebook.com/lolo.smith.169405 or Instagram @lolosmith2016.

Carla A. Nordé was born and raised in the District of Columbia. After graduating from Wilson Senior High school, she worked for several years then matriculated at Trinity University for three years. She now provides consulting services to non-profits that use the arts to enhance the life success of children and youth. She is the single mother of two children, a son and daughter. She helped write this book in response to her son being bullied at school. She has written two other books, *Be A Superhero By Standing Up Against Bullying* and the Amazon #1 Bestseller *Superheroes Fight Bullying With Kindness* with LoLo Smith.

ABOUT THE PHOTOGRAPHER

Tep Gardner is an award-winning photographer with 45 years of experience. He is a green screen expert who specializes in portraits, special events and fashion shoots. Contact him at 202.239.0643 or email: tepentertainment@gmail.com.

ABOUT THE DESIGNER

Gloria Marconi is an illustrator and graphic designer who has been working in the Washington, DC area for nearly 50 years. A multi-faceted artist, Ms. Marconi specializes in print and works in a variety of media ranging from traditional to quilting to computer-generated illustration. Over the years, her clients have run the gamut from corporations to government to non-profits as well as editorial illustrations for books, magazines and advertising. She lives in suburban Maryland and can be reached at gmarconidesign@verizon.net.

45